Wonderful WORLD 2

WORKBOOK

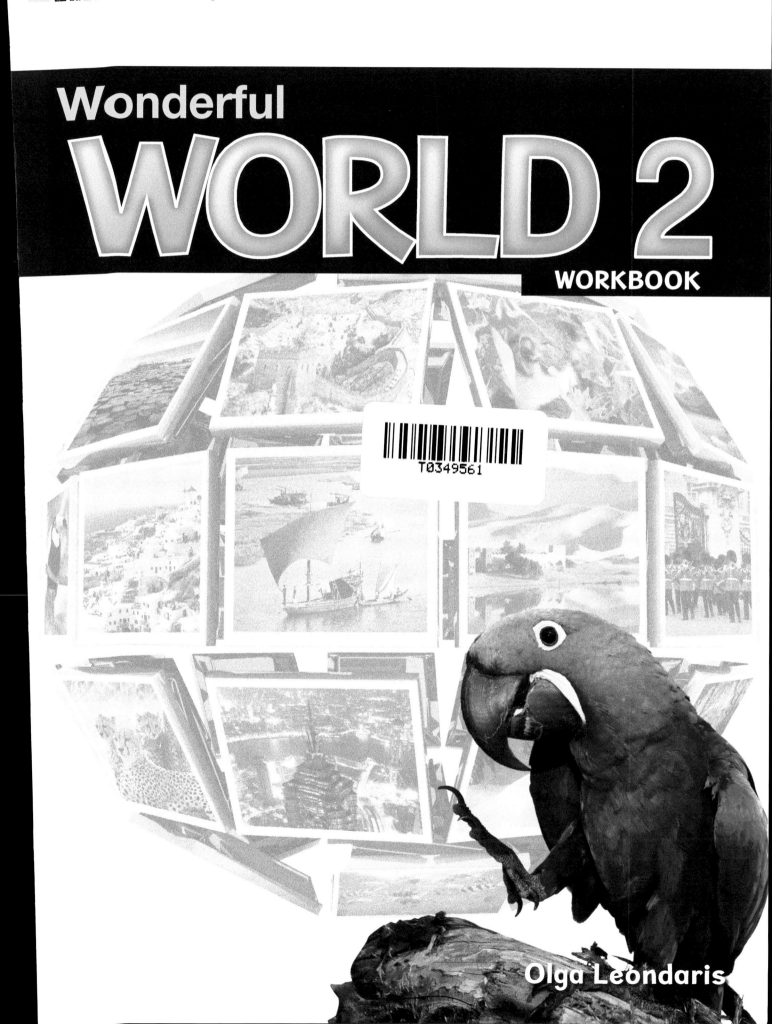

Olga Leondaris

NATIONAL GEOGRAPHIC LEARNING | CENGAGE Learning·

Wonderful World 2 Workbook
Olga Leondaris

Publisher: Jason Mann

Director of Content Development: Sarah Bideleux

Commissioning Editor: Carol Goodwright

Development Editor: Lynn Thomson

Assistant Editor: Manuela Barros

Content Project Editor: Amy Smith

Production Controller: Denise Power

Art Director/Cover designer: Natasa Arsenidou

Text designer: Tania Diakaki

Compositor: Rouli Manias

National Geographic Editorial Liaison: Leila Hishmeh

Illustrators: George Melissaropoulos, Theodoros Piakis
    and Panagiotis Angeletakis

For permission to use material from this text or product,
submit all requests online at **www.cengage.com/permissions**

Further permissions questions can be emailed to
permissionrequest@cengage.com

ISBN: 978-1-111-40205-1

National Geographic Learning
Cheriton House, North Way, Andover, Hampshire, SP10 5BE
United Kingdom

Cengage Learning is a leading provider of customized learning solutions with office locations around the globe, including Singapore, the United Kingdom, Australia, Mexico, Brazil and Japan. Locate your local office at:
international.cengage.com/region

Cengage Learning products are represented in Canada by
Nelson Education, Ltd.

Visit National Geographic Learning online at **ngl.cengage.com**

Visit our corporate website at **www.cengage.com**

Acknowledgements

The publisher would like to thank the following sources for permission to reproduce their copyright protected photos:

Cover: Left to right, top to bottom: Jim Richardson/National Geographic Image Collection, George Steinmetz/ National Geographic Image Collection, Medford Taylor/ National Geographic Image Collection, David Edwards/National Geographic Image Collection, Eduardo Rivero/Shutterstock Images, Richard Nowitz/National Geographic Image Collection, Dick Durrance II/National Geographic Image Collection, Guy Needham/National Geographic Image Collection, Scott S. Warren/National Geographic Image Collection, Michael Poliza/National Geographic Image Collection, Fritz Hoffmann/National Geographic Image Collection. Parrot: Creatista/Shutterstock.

Inside: iStockphoto - pp 31 (Matka Wariatka), 34 (Elkor), 70 (Kevin Klopper, Christian Wheatley), 73 (Michael DeLeon), 81 (anouchka, nautilus_shell_studios); National Geographic - pp65 (Randy Olson) p67 (Joel Sartore); Photolibrary Group - p 64 (Pixtal Images); Shutterstock - pp 7 (Eric Isselée x 3, Hans Meerbeek, Valua Vitaly, Florian Ispas), p8 (Dusan Jankovic, stocknadia, Brendan Howard, apdesign, Binkski), 10 (Monkey Business Images, Eric Isselée, Konstantin Shevtsov), 12 (E. Spek, Dmitriy Shironosov, Yuri Arcurs, Nikita Rogul, Dusan Zidar, Yuri Arcurs), 13 (Sonya Etchison, Yuri Arcurs), 14 (Nessli Orpmas, Deniz Ünlüsü, Adam Gryko, joyfuldesigns, Joe Gough, Tatiana Morozova), 15 (Kokhanchikov, Zurijeta, Muellek Josef, Bronwyn Photo, Cheryl Casey), 16 (ene, beltsazar, V. J. Matthew, Bull's-Eye Arts, Sarah Holmlund), 18 (Marie C Fields, Pavel Pustina, Anna Omelchenko, Sinisa Botas), 19 (Monika Wisniewska), 19 (spe, Kulish Viktoria, Lim Yong Hian, Civdis, Yan Ke), 20 (Fernando Blanco Calzada, Dmitry Fisher, Nailia Schwarz, Villedieu Christophe, Margo Harrison), 21 (0833379753, Serg64, Tissiana Bowman, Angela Luchianiuc, Ugorenkov Aleksandr, Eric Isselée), 23 (Andreja Donko, Arkady, Phase4Photography, EcoPrint, markiss, Pablo Scapinachis), 24 (Dmitry Naumov, Shebeko, Karkas, Andrey Armyagov, Angelo Gilardelli, Polina Lobanova), 26 (Photoaloja, Andrey Kozachenko, Andrew McDonough, Jeff Thrower, Dmitriy Karelin, David Koscheck,tezzstock,Marie C Fields, Vinicius Tupinamba x2), 27 (Monkey Business Images, fstockfoto, wavebreakmedia ltd, Linn Currie, studiots, Hannamariah), 28 (Monkey Business Images, Lorraine Swanson, Edw, Mandy Godbehear, Emin Kuliyev), 29 (Jody Dingle, Mark Breck, Mandy Godbehear, Monkey Business Images), 31 (Edyta Pawlowska, Peter Kirillov, Timofeyev Alexander, prodakszyn, Monkey Business Images), 33 (Zurijeta, Archana Bhartia, Yurchyks, Andrejs Pidjass, ruzanna, Emin Ozkan), 34 (Henrik Winther Andersen, Andrea Haase, Alexandru Chiriac, Margreet van der Voort), 39 (Piligrim), 40 (7505811966, Andrew Thomas, fotosav x 2, Olga Miltsova, Rago Arts), 42 (Aleksandr Stennikov, Iakov Kalinin), 43 (Nagy Melinda, mashe, Adna, Gladskikh Tatiana, grivet, Anyka, Enrico Jose), 44 (Edyta Pawlowska, Nayashkova Olga, Monkey Business Images, Lepas), 47 (oku, Georgios Kollidas), 48 (Inga Nielsen), 49 (Monkey Business Images, ArrowStudio, LLC, Maksim Shmeljov, cloki x 2, trubach, STILLFX, Gemenacom, Verisakeet), 52 (Andrew Doran, Lisa F. Young, EML, haider, Monkey Business Images, Orange Line Media), 53 (Suzanne Tucker, Monkey Business Images), 54 (Jorge Salcedo, Vibrant Image Studio, Veronika Vasilyuk, Oleg Zabielin, briedis), 56 (Konstantin Sutyagin, Morgan Lane Photography, Picsfive, MaszaS, Alex Staroseltsev), 58 (2happy, kbremote, Christoph Weihs, Alexander Ishchenko, Jozef Sedmak, Utekhina Anna), 59 (Andreka, Nikolai Tsvetkov, Gorilla, Thomas M Perkins, Petro Feketa, Ian Scott), 60 (Philip Lange, Mr Doomits, Andresr, Farferros, Bortel Pavel), 64 (holligan78, tatniz, Michael-John Wolfe, Media Union), 65 (Melanie DeFazio, Monkey Business Images, aleks.k), 67 (Norman Chan), 68 (Valentyn Volkov, Studio Araminta, objectsforall, Tupungato, E.G.Pors), 69 (Morgan Lane Photography), 70 (Philip Lange, Luciano Mortula, Seleznev Oleg, Anita Colic), 72 (Brandon Seidel, Carsten Reisinger, Dusan Po, Stephen Finn, Jim Barber, Liv Friis-Larsen), 73 (MaszaS, Monkey Business Images,Alex James Bramwell, wrangler, fcarucci), 76 (Subbotina Anna), 78 (Anna Galejeva, Losevsky Pavel, fcarucci, Iakov Kalinin, Jean Frooms, FuzzNails), 79 (sianc), 80 (3dimentii); Thinkstock - pp 40 (iStockphoto), 44 (iStockphoto), 47 (iStockphoto), 49 (iStockphoto), 67 (Jupiterimages).

Printed in the United Kingdom by Ashford Colour Press
Print Number 12 Print Year 2019

Contents

Page

Hello!	4
Happy Trails! Trek and his Reporters	7
Unit 1	8
Unit 2	14
Unit 3	20
Review 1	26
Unit 4	28
Unit 5	34
Unit 6	40
Review 2	46
Unit 7	48
Unit 8	54
Unit 9	60
Review 3	66
Unit 10	68
Unit 11	74
Unit 12	80
Review 4	86
Wordsearches	88
Jigsaws	95

A Look and write.

 A a    B b    _C_ c    D __

 E e    F f    __ g    H h

 I __    __ j    K k    L l

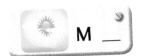 M __    N n    O o    __ p

 Q q    R __    S s    __ t

 U u    V __    W w    X x

 __ y    Z __

B Read and colour.

1  red

2 black

3 green

4  pink

5 orange

6  blue

7 brown

8 purple

9 yellow

10 white

4

A Write.

1
M o n d a y

2
Tu __ s _____

3
W __ dn __ s _____

4
T __ ur_____

5
F__ i _____

6
S ___ ur_____

7
S__ n _____

B Write.

I'm f o u r teen.

1

We're th ___ t ___ n.

2

We're e ___ ven.

3

I'm n _ _ _.

4

I'm tw _____ y.

5

I'm ___ x.

6

C Match and say.

What's your name?

How old are you?

How are you?

Fine, thanks.

My name's Anna.

I'm twelve.

Hello!

A Write.

baby   child   ~~foot~~   penguin   snake   tomato

1

foot   feet

4

_____   _____

2

_____   _____

5

_____   _____

3

_____   _____

6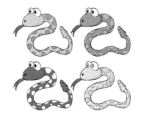

_____   _____

B Circle.

1
This / **These** apples are red!

4
These / Those cars are fantastic!

2
Those / That parrots are beautiful!

5
This / That isn't my football!

3
That / This robot is cool!

6
Those / That is my grandpa.

A **Write and say.**

boy   Dina   fox   Leo   leopard   meerkat   Mia   panda   Trek   Ty

Hello, I'm _____Trek_____ .
I'm a _____boy_____ .

I'm _____ .
I'm a _____ .

Hi, I'm _____ .
I'm a _____ .

Hello, I'm _____ .
I'm a _____ .

Hello, I'm _____ .
I'm a _____ .

B **Write.**

1 L
E
2 F O
P
3 M   4 B   A
5 R _ _ _ _ _ R
D
6 P _ _ _

7

A **Circle.**

camel / (email)

tea / stars

email / camel

sand / tea

stars / sand

B **Write.**

| camels | email | sand | ~~stars~~ | tea |

1 Look at the beautiful _____stars_____!
2 It's an _____ from Tina!
3 The trails are in the _____ .
4 Those _____ are from Morocco.
5 This _____ is very hot!

C **Circle.**

1 These camels (are) / is beautiful!
2 It are / is hot in the desert!
3 Anne and Sue are / is teachers.
4 I am / is a reporter.
5 This tea are / is for Harry.
6 You am / are my brother.
7 Hassan are / is my friend.
8 Dina am / is the new reporter.

D Write.

1   Ty, Leo, Mia and Dina are reporters.

   ____They're____ reporters.

2   The tea is hot.

   _____ hot.

3   The reporters are Trek's friends.

   _____ Trek's friends.

4   The email is from Dina.

   _____ from Dina.

5   Trek is Tessy's brother.

   _____ Tessy's brother.

6   Dina is the new reporter.

   _____ the new reporter.

E Write and say.

| camel   desert   riding   ~~sand~~   tea   tent   trails |

Trails in the ____sand____ .
   It's hot! It's hot!
   _____ in the sand.
   It's hot! It's hot.

A tent in the _____ .
   Tea for you and me!
A _____ in the desert.
   _____ for you and me!

Riding on a _____ .
In the desert! In the desert!
   _____ on a camel.
In the desert! In the desert!

A Write.

> aunt   cousins   forest   ~~photo~~   uncle

This is my favourite (1) ____photo____ .
The girls are Lucy and Sally. They are
my (2) _____ . Kate and John
are in the photo too. Kate's got long
hair. She's my (3) _____ . John
is my (4) _____ . He's nice!
Lucy, Sally, Kate and John are in the
(5) _____ .

B Write.

1 He's my mum's dad.   g r a n d p a
2 She's my dad's sister.   a _ _ _ _
3 He's my mum's brother.   u _ _ _ e
4 They're my aunt and uncle's children.   c _ _ _ _ _ s

C Write 'm not, aren't or isn't.

1 Jack and Jill _____aren't_____ cousins.
2 I _____ a baby.
3 The children _____ in a tent.
4 John _____ a teacher.
5 You _____ my aunt.
6 Kate _____ from America.
7 My dog _____ big.
8 The children _____ at school.

D **Write.**

1. 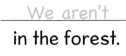 We aren't in the forest.

2. _____ my dad.

3. _____ seven years old.

4. _____ my aunt.

5. _____ a camel.

E **Read, draw and say.**

These aren't snakes.
They're lizards!

This isn't a hat.
It's a tent!

These aren't apples.
They're tomatoes!

That isn't my cousin in
the photo. It's me!

A Write.

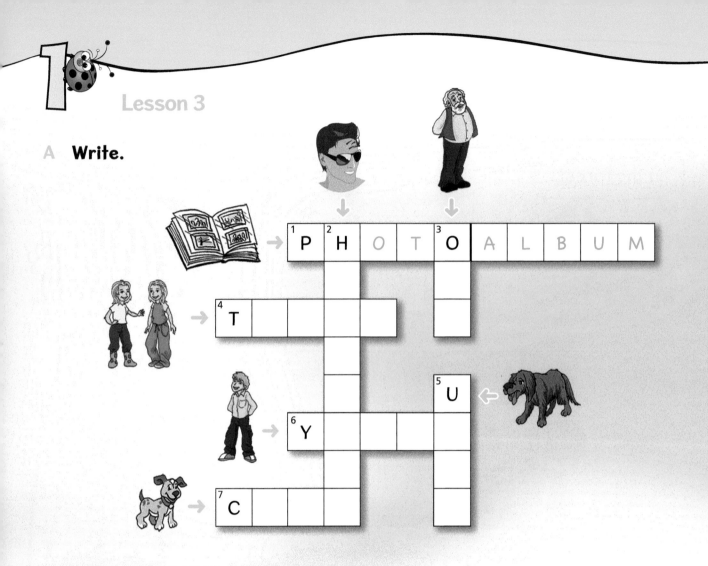

Crossword:
1 across: P H O T O A L B U M
4 across: T
6 across: Y
7 across: C
5 down: U

B Write.

cute   handsome   old   photo album   twins   ~~ugly~~

1

Is the dog
_____ugly_____?
Yes, it is.

2

Are Maria and Sara
_____?
Yes, they are.

3

Is Grandma
_____?
Yes, she is.

4

Is this your
_____?
Yes, it is.

5

Is the kitten
_____?
Yes, it is.

6

Is the man
_____?
Yes, he is.

C **Circle.**

1 Is this a photo album?
   Yes, I am / (it is).

2 Is this tea from Morocco?
   No, it isn't / they aren't.

3 Are those girls your cousins?
   Yes, she is / they are.

4 Is dad in the photo?
   Yes, he is / you are.

5 Is Harry handsome?
   No, he isn't / you aren't.

6 Is my teacher young?
   No, she isn't / we aren't.

D **Write.**

1 Are the boys young?
   Yes, they are.

2 Are the boys twins?
   _____

3 Is the dog cute?
   _____

4 Is the dog black?
   _____

E **Write and say.**

| aunt | beautiful | cousin | cute | old |
| ~~grandma and grandpa~~ | handsome | uncle | | |

This is my (3) _____,
Meg. She's (4) _____ .

This is my (1)
grandma and
grandpa .
They're nice, but
they're
(2) _____ .

This is my
(5) _____,
Steve. He's
(6) _____ .

This is my
(7) _____,
Laura. She's
(8) _____ .

2 Lesson 1

A Write.

1 p h o t o a l b u m
2 r _ _ _
3 t _ _ _ _ _ _
4 s _ _ _ _ _ _ _ _
5 l _ _ _ _
6 a _ _ _ _ _ _ _

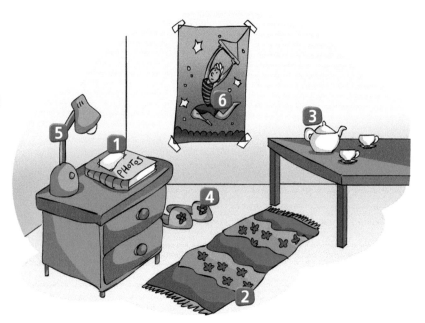

B Match.

This lamp is old.
That's a cool rug!
That's my mum's bag.
Those are beautiful slippers.
The acrobats are amazing!
That's my grandma's teapot.

C Write have got or has got.

1 I _____ have got _____ a great idea!
2 Liz and Susan _____ two cousins.
3 Tom _____ an amazing sister!
4 You _____ a cute cat.
5 Penny and I _____ blue bags.
6 My aunt _____ a nice teapot.
7 My dog _____ an old slipper.
8 Mum and Dad _____ a new rug.

D **Write.**

He's got   I've got   She's got   They've got   They've got   We've got

_____We've got_____ lots of flowers.

_____ a new lamp.

_____ cute twins!

_____ a new tent!

_____ new slippers.

_____ lots of rugs.

E **Write and say.**

Paul

Alice

Peter

Emily

Martin

Rachel

1   She's got a parrot.   _____It's Emily._____
2   He's got a cool hat.   _____
3   She's got a teapot.   _____
4   He's got a lizard.   _____
5   She's got flowers.   _____
6   He's got a tent.   _____

A Match.

canary
garden
goldfish
kitten
puppy
swing

B Write.

1 This is a baby dog.   p u p p y
2 This bird is small and yellow.   c _ _ _ _ _
3 This is a game for the garden.   s _ _ _ _
4 Lots of houses have got one of these.   g _ _ _ _ _
5 This is a baby cat.   k _ _ _ _ _
6 This fish is a pet.   g _ _ _ _ _ _ _

C Circle.

1 Our house haven't got / (hasn't got) a garden.
2 I haven't got / hasn't got any cousins.
3 Helen and James haven't got / hasn't got a goldfish.
4 You haven't got / hasn't got a photo album!
5 Rosie haven't got / hasn't got a brother.
6 We haven't got / hasn't got any pets.
7 William haven't got / hasn't got a dog.
8 The children haven't got / hasn't got a kitten.

D **Write.**

1 Wendy and I have got a puppy, but _____we haven't got a kitten_____ .
  (kitten)

2 I've got a nice house, but _____ . (car)

3 John's got a lovely garden, but _____ .
  (swing)

4 The desert has got lots of sand, but _____ .
  (lots of trees)

5 Lucy has got a brother, but _____ .
  (sister)

6 You have got a red hat, but _____ .
  (green hat)

7 I've got a canary, but _____ . (parrot)

8 Jill and Pam have got two aunts, but _____ .
  (an uncle)

E **Write and say.**

> bark   bird   canary   cat   chirp   dog
> ~~kitten~~   miaow   puppy   purr   tweet   yap

Purr like a _____kitten_____ .
Purr _____ purr!
Miaow like a _____ .
Miaow _____ miaow!

Yap like a _____ .
Yap _____ yap!
Bark like a _____ .
Bark _____ bark!

Tweet like a _____ .
Tweet _____ tweet!
Chirp like a _____ .
Chirp _____ chirp!

A Write.

B Write.

~~butterfly~~ fur horn leopard rhino shell snail ~~wings~~

1 This ___butterfly___ has got two beautiful ___wings___ .

2 This _____ has got yellow and black _____ .

3 This _____ has got a _____ .

4 This _____ has got a _____ .

18

C Match.

1 Have you got a brother?
2 Have elephants got wings?
3 Has Tara got a yellow canary?
4 Have you got a pet?
5 Has the acrobat got a hat?
6 Has the snail got a brown shell?

a No, she hasn't.
b Yes, I have.
c Yes, he has.
d Yes, it has.
e No, they haven't.
f No, we haven't.

D Write have, haven't, has or hasn't.

1 _____Has_____ the island got a forest?
   No, it _____hasn't_____ .

2 _____ whales got fur?
       No, they _____ .

3 _____ your garden got a swing?
   Yes, it _____ .

4 _____ Mary and Matthew got pets?
   Yes, they _____ .

5 _____ you got a goldfish?
   No, I _____ .

6 _____ Jenny got a brother?
   Yes, she _____ .

E Read, write and say.

1 It hasn't got fur, but it's got blue wings.   _____It's a butterfly._____

2 It hasn't got wings. It's got black and
   white fur.   _____

3 It's small and it's got orange fur.   _____

4 It hasn't got fur or legs. It's green.   _____

5 It's big. It hasn't got legs and it hasn't
   got fur.

3 Lesson 1

A Circle and write.

c b e n c h y b d o o r x c w w a l l v t u f o u n t a i n a b w m p 3 p l a y e r d p l

1 _____bench_____

2 _____

3 _____   4 _____   5 _____

B Write.

1 I've got a new ___MP3 player___ .

2 This  _____ is beautiful.

3 This  _____ is very old.

4 That house has got a blue  _____ .

5 There's a new  _____ in the park.

C Write.

1   This is _____my_____ kitten. (I)
2   Is _____ uncle very young? (you)
3   The dog is ugly, but _____ fur is nice. (it)
4   Are the twins in _____ tent? (they)
5   They have got _____ books. (we)
6   Is this _____ mobile phone? (you)

D Match and write.

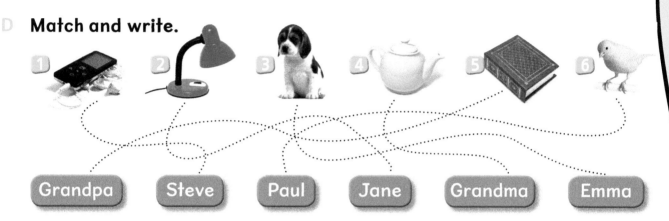

1   Grandpa   Steve   Paul   Jane   Grandma   Emma

1   Whose MP3 player is it?   _It's Steve's MP3 player._
2   Whose lamp is it?   _____
3   Whose puppy is it?   _____
4   Whose teapot is it?   _____
5   Whose photo album is it?   _____
6   Whose canary is it?   _____

E Write and say.

camels   markets   Morocco's
~~name~~   walls   world

Come on everybody.
My _____name_____ is Ty.
I'm a reporter.
All around the _____
I report!

Deserts and _____ .
Castles and _____.
_____ and slippers.
_____ got them all.

21

A **Write.**

B **Write.**

1   The desk is b _e t w e e n_ the two windows.

2   The kitten is n _ _ _ _ the toy box.

3   There is a rug on the f _ _ _ _ _ near the bed.

4   There are lots of toys in the t _ _ _   _ _ _ _.

5   The desk is m _ _ _ _ _ _!

22

C **Write There is, There isn't, There are or There aren't.**

 _____There isn't_____ a fountain in the park.

 _____ lots of books on the desk.

 _____ any drawings on the wall.

 _____ a canary in the tree.

 _____ any girls in the photo.

 _____ a shop on the island.

D **Write.**

1 _____Is there_____ a dress on the bed? Yes, _____there is_____ .
2 _____ photos in the book? No, _____ .
3 _____ camels in the desert? Yes, _____ .
4 _____ a MP3 player on the table? No, _____ .
5 _____ notebooks in your bag? No, _____ .
6 _____ a toy box in the bedroom? Yes, _____ .

E **Read and draw.**

This is my bedroom. There's a toy on the bed and there's a rug on the floor. There are two drawings on the wall and there are four books on the desk. There are two slippers under the desk.

23

A Write.

c _a_ _f_ _é_

_ w _ a _ e _

c _ _ _ _

_ r _ _ s _ _ s

_ _ o _ e _

b _ _ _ _

B Write.

1 Whose ____coat____ is this?

2 My _____ are red.

3 Is this your _____?

4 These  _____ are long.

5 John's got a new, blue  _____ .

6 There's a  _____ . Let's have a drink!

C Circle.

1 There's (a) / the nice café near my house.

2 I'm in a / the clothes shop. A / The shop's got beautiful dresses.

3 He's got an / the old coat and he wants a / the new coat.

4 A / The sky isn't very blue today.

5 It's a / the lovely jacket, but it isn't new.

6 Harry is a / an acrobat, he isn't a / an reporter.

D Circle and match.

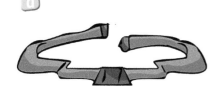

1 There's (a) / an café!   [f]

2 An / The car is fantastic!   [ ]

3 There's a / an orange belt.   [ ]

4 That is a / an yellow coat.   [ ]

5 An / The boat is big!   [ ]

6 There's a bird in a / the sky!   [ ]

E Match and say.

1 Look! Stars!   a The scarf is long.

2 Look! Boots!   b The toy shop is next to the café.

3 Look! A scarf!   c The stars are in the sky.

4 Look! Clothes!   d The clothes are new.

5 Look! A toy shop!   e The boots are black.

Review 1

Units 1-3

A **Write.**

B **Circle.**

1 This is my MP3 player / (cousin), John.

2 Are they your acrobat / gloves? Yes, they are.

3 The rhino has got a big wing / horn.

4 There's a leopard / teapot on the table.

5 They've got a swing / rug in their garden.

6 There's a rug on the floor / window.

7 Has Dan got a pet lamp / goldfish?

8 There's an email / puppy for you on the computer.

C **Write.**

They _____aren't_____ young.

Is the coat red? Yes, it _____ .

My cousins _____ ugly. They're cute!

Are they tired? Yes, they _____ .

My bedroom _____ messy.

Our garden _____ amazing!

D **Write.**

1 ___Have___ you ___got___ a teapot? No, ___I haven't___ .
2 Katie _____ (✗) a kitten. She's got a goldfish.
3 Ben _____ (✔) a belt. It's black.
4 I _____ (✔) a photo album. It's big.
5 _____ Harry _____ a sweater? Yes, _____ .
6 A bird _____ (✗) a shell. It's got wings.

E **Write.**

1 is / belt / whose / this / ? ___Whose belt is this?___
2 my / MP3 player / this / is _____
3 nice / this / coat / a / is _____
4 a / book / there's / the / on / bed _____
5 café / my / big / uncle's / is _____

F **Read and draw. Then say.**

This is my bedroom.
There's _____
There are _____

A Write.

|¹S| | | |
|K| |²S|
³I								
			⁵F
⁴T			

B Circle and write.

1. Lara is
___skiing___.

2. They're a great
_____!

pskiingmwteamvpsicehockeyloqfreezingucshoutrngpomfallingts

3. _____
is fun!

4. She's
_____ .

5. Let's
_____!

6. Oh no! She's
_____!

28

C Circle.

1   I 're / **'m** studying in my bedroom.

2   Grandma 's / 'm listening to my music!

3   They 'm / 're shouting at those children.

4   Mum 's / 're having fun!

5   Hooray! We 's / 're winning!

6   You 's / 're sleeping in my sleeping bag!

D Write.

We _'re looking_____ (look) at clothes.

The cat _____ _____ (sleep) on my bed!

The children _____ _____ (have) a lot of fun!

He _____ (laugh)!

Oh no! The teapots _____ (fall).

Dad _____ _____ (take) a photo.

E Write and say.

Peter

Alison

Steve

Liz   Mark

Mandy

1   Who's listening to music?   _Steve's listening to music._

2   Who's watching TV?   _____

3   Who's skiing?   _____

4   Who's playing ice hockey?   _____

5   Who's doing homework?   _____

6   Who's riding a bike?   _____

29

A **Write.**

1 Jan <u>u a r</u> y

2 Fe _____ ry

3 M _____

4 ___ ril

5 __ a __

6 J _____

7 _____ y

8 A _____ st

9 S ___ t _____

10 _____ ber

11 Nov _____

12 D _____ ber

B **Write.**

Spring

_____
April
_____

Summer

_____
_____
August

Autumn

_____
October
_____

Winter

December
_____
_____

30

C Circle.

(I'm not) / You aren't **standing.**

Dad isn't / aren't **reading a book.**

Maya isn't / aren't **snowboarding.**

We isn't / aren't **eating oranges.**

Bill isn't / aren't **studying.**

They isn't / aren't **sleeping.**

D Write.

1 Lucy's sitting on the chair. _____She isn't sitting_____ on the desk.

2 We're skiing in Canada. _____ in England.

3 I'm studying in my bedroom. _____ in the kitchen.

4 The dog is swimming in the river. _____ in the sea.

5 You're going to school. _____ to the park.

6 They are playing basketball. _____ ice hockey.

E Write and say.

_____January_____, _____, _____.

Clap your hands for _____!

_____, _____, _____.

Stamp your feet for _____!

_____, _____,

And _____ too.

Say hooray for _____!

HOORAY!

Lesson 3

A Write.

1 The children like
   c _a m p i n g_ .

2 They're camping near
   a v _ _ _ _ _ _ _ .

3 The t _ _ _ _ is blue.

4 The children are sitting
   around a f _ _ _ _ .

5 They are cooking
   b _ _ _ _ _ _ _ .

6 There are three
   s _ _ _ _ _ _ _ _ b _ _ _ _ .

B Write.

camping fire burgers sleeping tent ~~village~~

1 He's staying in a lovely _____ _village_ _____ .

2 The twins are _____ in one sleeping bag!

3 Sally's on a _____ holiday with her mum.

4 They're eating _____ in the garden!

5 We're sleeping in our new _____ .

6 I'm freezing! Let's sit near the _____ .

C Match.

1 Are you shopping in the market?

2 Is your dad sleeping in the tent?

3 Is your mum reading her book?

4 Are the children eating?

5 Are you dancing?

6 Are Andy and Kate listening
  to music?

a Yes, they are. They're hungry!

b Yes, he is. He's tired.

c No, we aren't. We're in a shop.

d Yes, we are. We're having fun.

e No, she isn't. She's sleeping.

f No, they aren't. They're
  watching TV.

D Write.

_____Are_____ they _____sleeping_____ (sleep) in the tent?
_No, they aren't._____

_____ you _____ (ride) your bike?
_____

_____ Alice _____ (take) a photo?
_____

_____ John _____ (win) the game?
_____

_____ the cats _____ (eat)?
_____

_____ he _____ (have) fun?
_____

E Match and say.

1 What are you doing?

2 What is Thomas doing?

3 What are the children doing?

4 What is Mum doing?

5 What is the dog doing?

a He's sleeping in the tent.

b It's swimming in the river.

c They're staying with their grandma and grandpa.

d I'm sitting near the fire.

e She's cooking burgers.

Lesson 1

A Match.

speak

ice

hotel

country

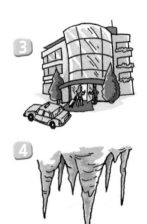

B Write.

country   French   ~~hotel~~   ice   warm

Bonjour!

We're staying in this beautiful ____hotel____ .

Canada is a big _____ .

Marie can speak _____ .

The tea isn't hot or cold. It's _____!

It's freezing! There's _____ on the river.

C Match.

1 John can't watch TV.   a It's time for bed.
2 I can see the mountains!   b But she can't climb trees.
3 We can't go to the beach.   c There's ice on the floor.
4 Lara can ride a bike.   d It's raining!
5 I can't stand up!   e They're beautiful!

D **Write.**

1. _Can_ Hilda _ski_ ? (ski)
   Yes, she can.

2. _____ we _____ at this hotel? (stay)
   _____

3. _____ George's father _____? (cook)
   _____

4. _____ they _____ tea? (make)
   _____

5. _____ Victor _____ ice hockey? (play)
   _____

6. _____ Jenny _____? (snowboard)
   _____

E **Write about you. Then say.**

1. speak English   _I can speak English._
2. climb a tree   _____
3. swim   _____
4. ride a bike   _____
5. ski   _____
6. speak French   _____

5 Lesson 2

A Write.

B Write **must** or **mustn't**.

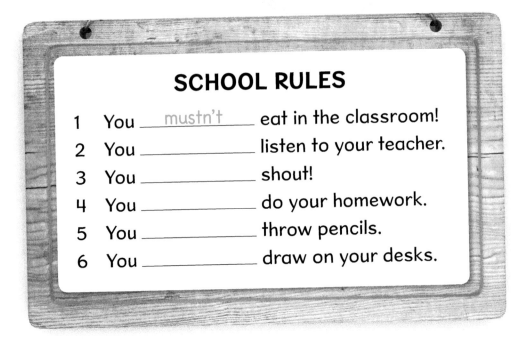

SCHOOL RULES

1 You ___mustn't___ eat in the classroom!
2 You _____ listen to your teacher.
3 You _____ shout!
4 You _____ do your homework.
5 You _____ throw pencils.
6 You _____ draw on your desks.

C **Circle.**

1 My (baseball cap) / trainers is green.
2 They're winning! They're running high / fast.
3 Catch / Throw the ball! I'll catch it.
4 Ice hockey isn't a slow / throw sport.
5 Look at number nine! He can jump slow / high.
6 My dog can catch / throw balls.
7 Jim's got new baseball cap / trainers.
8 Tennis, basketball and baseball are sports / trainers.

D **Match.**

1 We mustn't talk to our friends.   a It's freezing today!
2 We must wear gloves.   b We must walk.
3 We mustn't throw the ball.   c We must listen to our teacher.
4 We mustn't run.   d We must study.
5 We can't watch TV.   e We must kick it!

E **Write and say.**

down   fast   high   shorts   slow   ~~sports~~   sports   trainers   up

It's time for ___sports___ !
Put on your _____ ,
and your _____ too!

You must run _____ .
You mustn't be _____ .
You must jump _____ .
        There you go!

♪ Sit _____ .
   Stand _____ .
        Run and jump.

Come on boys and girls!
It's time for _____ !

37

A Match.

third   fifth   eighth   sixth   tenth

1st   2nd   3rd   4th   5th   6th   7th   8th   9th   10th

fourth   first   second   ninth   seventh

B Write.

1 Darren's ___seventh___ .

2 Harold's _____ .

3 Laura's _____ .

4 Anna's _____ .

5 Mary's _____ .

6 Kate's _____ .

7 Basil's _____ .

8 Peter's _____ .

9 Fiona's _____ .

10 Sally's _____ .

C Match.

1 Be quiet!
2 Don't run!
3 Read this book.
4 Let's go to the park.
5 Don't shout, children.
6 Let's look in the shop.

a It's great.
b It's got nice clothes.
c The baby is sleeping!
d This is a library.
e We can play on the swings.
f There's lots of ice!

D Write.

1 Sleep in a sleeping bag. _____Don't sleep_____ on the floor.
2 Don't stay in a hotel. _____ with your friends.
3 Write in your notebook. _____ on the wall!
4 Speak English. _____ French.
5 Don't sit on your desk. _____ on your chair.
6 Throw the ball. _____ the sandwich!

E Write and say.

1 The _____first_____ pencil is red.
2 The _____ pencil is blue.
3 The _____ pencil is white.
4 The _____ pencil is black.
5 The _____ pencil is brown.
6 The _____ pencil is green.
7 The _____ pencil is yellow.
8 The _____ pencil is orange.
9 The _____ pencil is pink.
10 The _____ pencil is purple.

6 Lesson 1

A Circle.

1 

th i r s t y

2 

o ______ j __ce

3 

g ____

4 

w _____f ___

5 

l _____ad _

6 

w _____

7 

t _____

8 

s _______ch

B Write.

grass lemonade orange juice pizza table thirsty ~~waterfall~~

This family is having a picnic. They aren't sitting near the (1) waterfall. The (2) ____________ is wet. They are sitting at the (3) ____________ under the tree. The children are hungry and (4) ____________. What can they eat? There are sandwiches and (5) ____________ too. What can they drink? There is (6) ____________ and (7) ____________.

C Circle.

1 I'm hungry! Have we got some / (any) sandwiches?

2 There are some / any tables, but there aren't some / any chairs!

3 Is there some / any lemonade? No, but we've got some / any orange juice.

4 Are there some / any book shops in the town?

5 There are some / any trainers on the floor.

6 This country's got some / any beautiful beaches! Are there some / any nice hotels?

D Write some or any.

1 Are there _____any_____ cakes on the table?

   Yes, there are _____some_____ cakes on the table.

2 Has she got _____ brothers or sisters?

   No, she hasn't got _____ brothers or sisters.

3 Are there _____ books on the shelf?

   No, there aren't _____ books on the shelf.

4 Have they got _____ new boys in their team?

   Yes, they've got _____ new boys in their team.

5 Are there _____ nice drawings in our classroom?

   Yes, there are _____ nice drawings in our classroom.

6 Is there _____ water in the fountain?

   Yes, there is _____ water in the fountain.

E Write, colour and say.

We have f u n in J __ ne and J __ ly! We have l __ nch __ nder the s __ n.

A Write.

20 t<u>w e n</u>ty

30 t_____y

40 f____y

50 f_f___

60 s___ t_

70 s_____ty

80 e____ t_

90 n_____y

100 o___ h___d____

B Write.

eighty   fifty   forty   ninety   one hundred   seventy   sixty   thirty   ~~twenty~~

20 _____twenty_____   50 _____   80 _____

30 _____   60 _____   90 _____

40 _____   70 _____   100 _____

C Write.

~~apple~~   ~~chocolate~~   ice cream   juice   lemonade
orange   sandwich   burger   sugar   water

How much ...?
____chocolate____
_____
_____
_____
_____

How many ...?
____apples____
_____
_____
_____
_____

D **Write.**

child   ice   ice cream   month   ~~photo~~   sugar   sweet   tent

How many _photos_ are there?

_____ are there?

_____ can we buy?

_____ is there?

_____ do you want?

_____ are there?

_____ have they got?

_____ can you eat?

E **Write and say.**

black   blue   brown   green   orange   pink   purple   ~~red~~   white   yellow

10   20   30   40   50
60   70   80   90   100

Ten is _____red_____ .   Sixty is _____ .
Twenty is _____ .   Seventy is _____ .
Thirty is _____ .   Eighty is _____ .
Forty is _____ .   Ninety is _____ .
Fifty is _____ .   One hundred is _____ .

A **Write.**

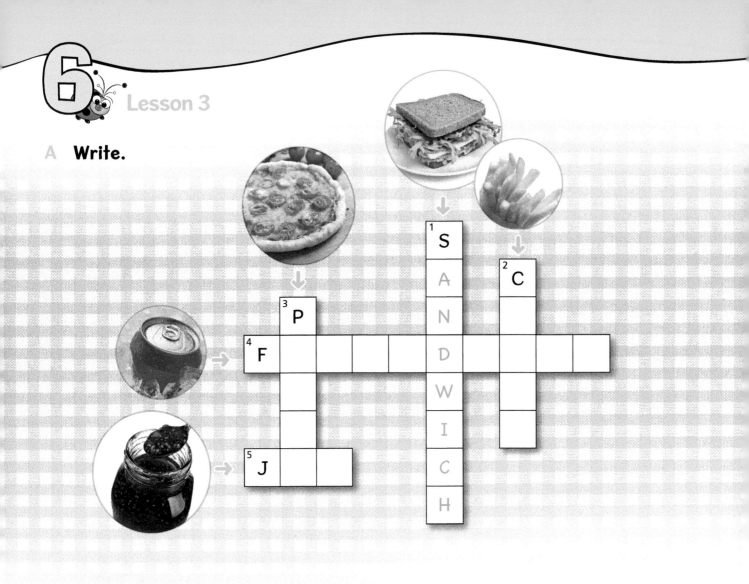

B **Write.**

1 There's lots of chocolate on my birthday  _____cake_____ .

2 I like cheese and tomato on my  _____ .

3 Drink juice! Don't drink  _____ .

4 He's got lots of _____ in his sandwich.

5 I'm eating burgers and  _____ .

C Write.

her   him   it   ~~me~~   them   us   you

I	me
you	
he	
she	
it	
we	
they	

D Write.

1 Let's send John an email.
Let's send ___him___ an email.

2 Let's buy Grandma a present.
Let's buy _____ a present.

3 Look at the dog!
Look at _____ !

4 Let's send Mark and Tim some photos.
Let's send _____ some photos.

5 Don't throw the ball.
Catch _____!

6 Look at me and Steve.
Look at _____ .

E Match and say.

1 Can we have lots of lemonade?
2 It's Martha's birthday!
3 I have a new MP3 player!
4 I can't talk to Thomas.
5 Lisa and Kelly are good friends.

a Wow! Can I see it?
b Yes, we can. But it isn't good for us.
c Yes, they are. Everybody likes them.
d No, you can't. But you can send him an email.
e Let's buy her a nice present!

Review 2

A **Write.**

August   baseball cap   December   eighty   ~~fire~~   grass
ice hockey   January   May   one hundred   sixty   ski
sleeping bag   tent   thirty   trainers

Camping	Months	Numbers	Sports
fire			

B **Write.**

1 _____ grass _____
2 _____
3 _____
4 _____
5 _____
6 _____
7 _____
8 _____
9 _____
10 _____

C **Write.**

1 We _____'re eating_____ (eat) an ice-cream!

2 _____ (she / make) sandwiches? Yes, she is.

3 He _____ (not / do) his homework now.

4 I _____ (throw) the ball!

5 _____ (they / play) ice hockey? No, they aren't.

6 You _____ (not / stay) in the village.

46

D **Write must, mustn't, can or can't.**

You ____must____ study.

She _____ swim.

You _____ talk in a library!

Amy _____ stand!

E **Write.**

1 How (many) / much books are there on the shelf?

2 Are there any / some nice hotels in the village?

3 How many / much sugar do you want in your tea?

4 There are any / some French books in the library.

5 Are there any / some sleeping bags in the tent?

6 I want any / some burgers, please!

F **Write about you.**

1 Can you speak French? _____No, I can't._____

2 Can you play ice hockey? _____

3 Can you make a pizza? _____

4 Can you ski? _____

5 Can you run fast? _____

6 Can you jump high? _____

7 Can you catch a ball? _____

8 Can you make a sandwich? _____

A **Write.**

1 c <u>o o</u> k

2 p _ _ t _ _ r _ _ h _ r

3 _ _ c _ _ r

4 _ o _ _ m _ _ _

5 _ _ s _ _ i _

B **Write.**

> biscuits   cook   doctor   ~~photographer~~   postman

1 There are two reporters and one _photographer_ .
2 Help! Is there a _____ here?
3 The _____ makes amazing pizzas!
4 I want a _____ with my tea, please.
5 The _____ comes every morning.

C **Write.**

1 Penny _watches_ (watch) DVDs on Saturday.
2 Tim _____ (play) with his cousins on Sunday.
3 Emma _____ (go) to the library on Tuesday.
4 The postman _____ (ride) his bike every day.
5 Mum _____ (make) great biscuits!
6 Mr and Mrs Brown _____ (read) lots of books.

D **Circle.**

 They (study) / studies at school.

 John eat / eats biscuits every day!

 Mary play / plays the piano in the afternoon.

 We go / goes to the beach in the summer.

 The cat sleep / sleeps on my bed every night.

 Anne read / reads books on Saturday.

E **Write and say.**

| half past one | half past eleven | half past seven |
| ~~four o'clock~~ | nine o'clock | six o'clock |

 four o'clock

A **Write.**

	¹S	C	²A	R	³E	D

(crossword: 1-across S C A R E D; ⁴B across; with 2-down and 3-down columns)

B **Write.**

arrow   excited   ~~lesson~~   scared   teach

1. Is Jenny having a ___lesson___ now ?

2. I want a bow and _____!

3. Don't be _____!

4. Look! We're _____!

5. I _____ French at this school.

BONJOUR

C **Match.**

1 It's Saturday!

2 Mary likes cake.

3 Pete plays the guitar.

4 The acrobat's scared.

5 I'm not thirsty.

a She doesn't like biscuits.

b He doesn't want to fall.

c I don't want any lemonade.

d We don't have school!

e He doesn't play the drums.

D **Circle don't or doesn't.**

1 Simon don't / (doesn't) watch TV in the morning.

2 They don't / doesn't eat chips every day.

3 I don't / doesn't like dancing.

4 Grandma don't / doesn't go to school.

5 We don't / doesn't watch DVDs on Monday.

6 Uncle Paul don't / doesn't play the drums.

7 You don't / doesn't ride your bike to school.

8 Penny don't / doesn't read every night.

E **Write and say.**

~~excited~~   great   hooray   scared   stay

We are ___excited___!
Yes, we are.
We aren't scared!
No, we aren't.

Hip hip _____!
Today is a great day.
Hip hip hooray!
Today is a great day.

We are _____ .
Yes, we are.
We aren't excited.
No, we aren't.

Oh no! We can't _____ .
Today isn't a great day!
Oh no! We can't stay.
Today isn't a _____ day!

A Write.

actor   ~~astronaut~~   firefighter   pilot   police officer   vet

He walks on the moon.

__astronaut__

His job is dangerous.

_____

He flies an aeroplane.

_____

He's on TV.

_____

He helps animals.

_____

He helps with fires.

_____

B Circle.

1   Do /(Does) she work in a café?
    Yes, she do /(does.)

2   Do / Does you go to school in the morning?
    Yes, we do / does.

3   Do / Does they work at the weekend?
    No, they don't / doesn't.

4   Do / Does Mike read at night?
    Yes, he do / does.

5   Do / Does Susan have a lesson now?
    No, she don't / doesn't.

C **Match.**

actor   astronaut   firefighter   pilot   police officer   vet

D **Circle.**

	fizzy drinks	sport	BONJOUR	email
Peter	✔	✗	✔	✔
Anna	✗	✗	✗	✔

1 Does Peter like fizzy drinks?
   (a) Yes, he does.
   b No, he doesn't.

2 Does Anna speak French?
   a Yes, she does.
   b No, she doesn't.

3 Do Anna and Peter write emails?
   a Yes, they do.
   b No, they don't.

4 Does Peter speak French?
   a Yes, he does.
   b No, he doesn't.

5 Does Anna like fizzy drinks?
   a Yes, she does.
   b No, she doesn't.

6 Do Peter and Anna play sport?
   a Yes, they do.
   b No, they don't.

E **Join the dots. Then write and say.**

I'm Peter. I l _ _ e ani _ _ ls.
I w_ _ t to be a v _ t.

Lesson 1

A Circle.

1
cloudy / (sunny)

2
bridge / soldier

3
windy / rainy

4
umbrella / cloudy

5
bridge / umbrella

6
snowy / soldier

7
sunny / rainy

8
snowy / windy

B Circle and write.

frhumbrellaboosunnyarcloudywesoldierssyibridgeopnasnowyopip

1

Take your ___umbrella___ .
It's rainy!

2

Let's go to the beach.
It's _____!

3

Look! It's
_____!

4

He's a
_____ .

5

There's a
_____ .

6

It's _____!
Let's ski!

C   Write.

1   night / book / reads / Dad / a / sometimes / at

   <u>Dad sometimes reads a book at night.</u>

2   it / in / August / sunny / always / is

   _____

3   school / never / I / pizza / eat / at

   _____

4   January / often / is / in / cold / it

   _____

D   Write about you.

1   do homework

   <u>I always do my homework.</u>

2   go to the cinema

   _____

3   play ice hockey

   _____

4   swim in the sea

   _____

5   have pizza for lunch

   _____

E   Write and say.

It's a s <u>u</u> n <u>n</u> y day.
Let's go to the park and play.
It's a __ u __ n __ day.
Come on everybody!

It's a __ l __ u __ y day.
It's cold out there.
It's a c __ o __ d __ day.
Look at the sky everybody!

It's a r __ i __ y day.
It's wet out there.
It's a __ a __ n __ day.
Take your umbrellas everybody!

It's a w __ n __ y day.
Hats fly away.
It's __ i __ d __ day.
Hold your hats everybody!

It's a s __ o __ y day!
Let's go out and play. Hooray!
It's a __ n __ w __ day.
Come on everybody!

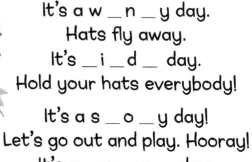

55

Lesson 2

A Find, circle and write.

S	N	O	W	M	A	N	G
E	W	J	O	C	O	P	F
K	A	S	R	B	C	N	Y
S	U	I	L	R	Z	H	M
E	K	I	D	S	P	E	P
G	H	L	U	W	R	A	P
C	X	B	B	E	W	D	S
L	B	U	T	T	O	N	E

1

_____head_____

2

_____

3

_____

4

_____

5

_____

B Write.

~~buttons~~   head   kids   snowman   world

1   There are five ____buttons____ on my coat.

2   The _____ is a big place.

3   Jane and Mark made a _____ in their garden.

4   Ben has a hat on his _____ .

5   The _____ visit their grandparents at the weekend.

C Match.

1   Pandas are

2   John's French is

3   The green buttons are

4   The boy's belt is

5   Lara's kittens are

a   nicer than his hat.

b   smaller than the red buttons.

c   better than his English.

d   cuter than the puppies.

e   fatter than giraffes.

Write.

> big   fat   ~~nice~~   old   warm   young

1

Cakes are __nicer than__ biscuits.

2

The boots are _____ the shoes.

3

Sarah is _____ than her brother.

4

Summer is _____ winter.

5

The black cat is _____ the white cat.

6

Grandpa is _____ Tom.

E   **Write and say.**

1   is / Vicky / than / shorter / Sissy   __Sissy is shorter than Vicky.__

2   Dan / Bill / is / than / taller   _____

3   happier / is / Vicky /Sissy / than   _____

4   than / longer / Sissy / hair / got / May / has   _____

_____

A **Write.**

1

s <u>c</u> a <u>r</u> y

2
s _ e _ p _

3

_ a _ g _

4

l _ t _ l _

5

_ a n _

B **Write.**

C Circle.

1 John is the (tallest) / taller child in the family.

2 This is the nicer / nicest hotel in town.

3 This is the yummiest / yummy cake at the party.

4 Fluffy is the cuter / cutest kitten in the world.

5 George is the worst / bad kid in school.

6 Pizzas are the better / best food.

D Write.

cold   cute   ~~good~~   scary   sleepy   tasty

Orange juice is the ___best___ drink.

Ben is the _____ puppy.

It's the _____ day of the year.

Ice cream is the _____ food.

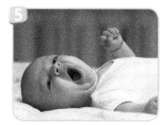

Peter is the _____ baby.

Sharks are the _____ animals.

E Read and draw. Then say.

This is a giraffe.
It's the tallest animal.
I think it's the best animal!

59

A **Write.**

1 m <u>u</u> s <u>e</u> u <u>m</u>

2 d _ n _ s _ u _

3 b _ n _

4 _ u _ e _

5 b _ g w _ e _ l

6 c _ o _ k

7 _ o _ k s _ o _

B **Circle and write.**

Let's go on the
___big wheel___! It's fun!

There's a _____
near my house.

Big Ben is a
_____ .

We were at a
_____ .

The _____
is scary.

That's a big
_____ .

C Circle.

1 I (was) / were at a bookshop last week.

2 The museum was / were fun!

3 We was / were in London on Saturday.

4 The big wheel was / were very high.

5 Johnny and Kate was / were at school yesterday.

6 Jackie was / were sleepy last night.

D Write.

It was   He was   She was   They were   ~~You were~~   We were

You were on holiday.

_____ my first piano lesson yesterday.

_____ in bed at 9 o'clock.

_____ at the park on Sunday.

_____ at the museum yesterday.

_____ on the rollercoaster.

E Write and colour. Then say.

The l __ on k __ ng and the wh __ te t __ ger sw __ m in spr __ ng.

Lesson 2

A Find, circle and write.

```
S  D  H  I  O  P  A  P
H  A  E  A  R  T  H  L
A  O  P  O  M  C  A  A
R  E  R  T  E  H  S  N
P  W  A  U  A  P  I  T
I  C  L  L  T  A  S  O
C  M  U  T  Y  D  Z  A
F  R  I  E  N  D  L  Y
```

earth _____   _____

_____   _____

_____

B Write.

earth   friendly   meat   ~~plant~~   sharp

1 I got Grandma a _____plant_____ for her birthday.
2 His teeth were _____ and dangerous.
3 I don't want _____ for dinner tonight, Mum!
4 Those kids are very _____ .
5 There are lots of amazing animals on _____ .

C Circle.

1 Mum (wasn't) / weren't at the house on Friday.
2 There wasn't / weren't a big wheel in the village.
3 The children wasn't / weren't scared of the dinosaur.
4 It wasn't / weren't a big bridge.
5 Pam wasn't / weren't at school today.
6 The firefighters wasn't / weren't very happy.

D **Write.**

1. The boys were / (weren't) at a museum.
   They (were) / weren't at a café.

2. Tina was / wasn't at the library.
   She was / wasn't at the beach.

3. They were / weren't at the park.
   They were / weren't at a party.

4. Rob and Simon were / weren't at school.
   They were / weren't at a bookshop.

5. I was / wasn't with my friends.
   I was / wasn't playing a computer game.

6. Mum and Carrie were / weren't on the big wheel.
   They were / weren't in the garden.

E **Write and say.**

| cutest   fast   forest   hungry   ~~sad~~   scary   smallest   strong |

Dino the dinosaur was very _____sad_____.
   He wasn't happy at all.
His friends were all big and _____.
   But he was small, small, small.

   Little Dino the dinosaur,
He was the _____ dinosaur of all!
   Little Dino the dinosaur,
He was the _____ dinosaur of all!

One day T-rex was in the _____.
   He was there behind a tree.
   He was big and _____!
   And he was very hungry!

   Little Dino was small and _____.
   He quickly climbed a tree.
Poor T-rex was _____ all day.
   But little Dino got away.

Lesson 3

A Match.

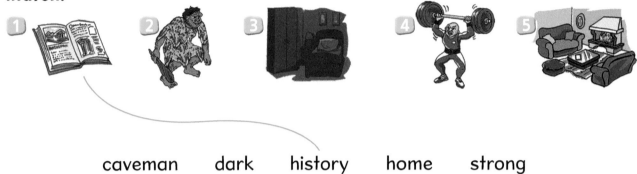

caveman   dark   history   home   strong

B Write.

caveman   dark   history   home   strong

caveman

_____

_____

_____

_____

C Circle and match.

1 (Was) / Were it hot in the summer?   a   Yes, he was.
2 Was / Were he a caveman?   b   Yes, we were.
3 Was / Were the buttons very small?   c   No, they weren't.
4 Was / Were Mum at home?   d   No, she wasn't.
5 Was / Were you at the supermarket   e   Yes, it was.
   yesterday?

D **Write was, wasn't, were or weren't.**

1 ___Were___ the cavemen strong? Yes, they ___were___ .

3 _____ the lesson about history? No, it _____ .

2 _____ the history book on the table? Yes, it _____ .

4 _____ they at home yesterday? No, they _____ .

E **Write and say.**

1 Was Jenny reading last night?
___Yes, she was.___

3 Were they at a museum yesterday?
_____

2 Were they in an art lesson?
_____

4 Was it dark at 7 o'clock?
_____

Review 3

A Find, circle and write.

T	K	B	A	U	D	N	P	V	W
F	H	O	S	B	O	H	W	S	A
C	F	S	T	P	C	S	I	H	C
H	D	N	R	I	T	W	N	R	T
X	A	O	O	L	O	I	D	A	O
P	R	W	N	O	R	S	Y	I	R
P	K	Y	A	T	R	U	I	N	N
C	L	O	U	D	Y	N	M	Y	K
P	O	S	T	M	A	N	G	U	H
C	O	O	K	C	F	Y	X	X	Q

Jobs

actor
_____
_____
_____
_____
_____

Weather

_____
_____
_____
_____
_____
_____

B Write.

1 big wheel
2 _____
3 _____
4 _____
5 _____
6 _____
7 _____
8 _____

C Circle.

1 Dinosaurs are (bigger) / biggest than flies.
2 Poppy is the prettier / prettiest girl in the class.
3 This café has the better / best ice cream ever!
4 Rob is taller / tallest than Mark.
5 August is warmer / warmest than November.

D Write.

1 _____Do_____ you like bookshops? No, ___I don't___ .
2 Jen _____ (not have) a history lesson today.
3 I _____ (like) snowboarding!
4 I _____ (want) some chips.
5 _____ Grandma watch TV? Yes, she _____ .

E Write.

_____Were_____ you at home
yesterday? ___Yes, we were___ .

It _____ rainy
this morning.

Kitty _____ at the
museum yesterday.

The cats _____ sleepy.

F Write about you.

I always _____ .

I sometimes _____ .

I often _____ .

I never _____ .

A **Write.**

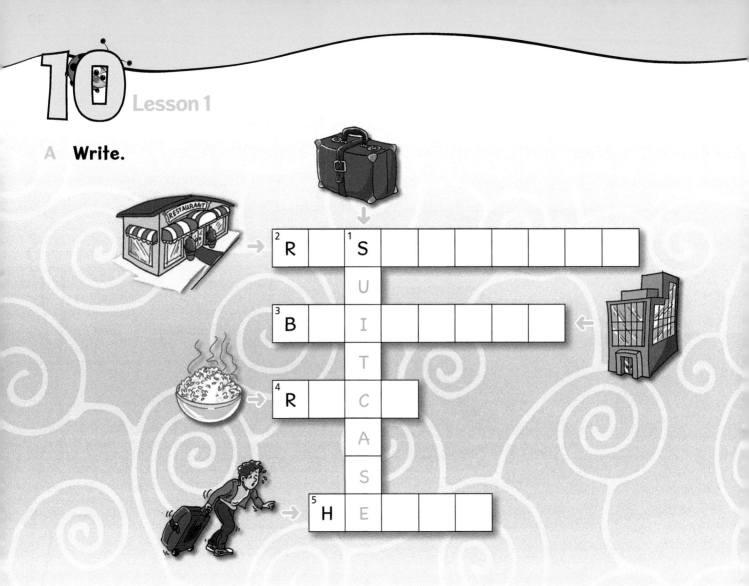

B **Circle.**

suitcase / (rice)

heavy / building

rice / suitcase

building / restaurant

restaurant / heavy

C **Write.**

This morning, I (1) ___packed___ (pack) my books in my schoolbag. When, I (2) _____ (carry) my bag to the door it was heavy!

(3) I _____ (wait) for the bus for 10 minutes. The bus (4) _____ (arrive) at 8 o'clock.

Twenty five minutes later, the bus
(5) _____(stop) at school and we
(6) _____ (jump) out. The bus driver
(7) _____ (shout) 'Have a nice day!' to us.

D **Write.**

> close   ~~cook~~   love   pack   stay

1   My mum ___cooked___ this pizza. It's yummy!
2   It's cold! I _____ the window.
3   Jenny _____ the cake we ate yesterday.
4   I _____ my bag. It's heavy!
5   Patty _____ with her cousin at the weekend.

E **Write and say.**

What can I eat in J a p a n?
Can I have ice cream or jam?
I don't know what to do!
What can I e _ t in Japan?

What can I eat in _ r _ e _ e?
Can I eat r _ c _ or fish?
I don't know what to do!
What can I eat in Greece?

Come on, everybody! Let's eat t _ g _ t _ e _!
Food from around the world!

S _ n _ w _ c _ e _, pizzas and rice.
Ice cream, j _ m and _ h _ c _ l _ t _ cake.
Come on, everybody! Let's eat together!
Food from around the world!

A **Match.**

Camels live in the desert.
I visited the pyramids!
Dad built a house in Greece.
We went to the cinema last week.

B **Write.**

> build   desert   ~~village~~   pyramid   last week

1   The houses in our _____village_____ are small.
2   John didn't have school _____ .
3   I _____ sandcastles on the beach.
4   It is hot in the _____ .
5   That _____ is very big.

C **Write.**

1   They _____built_____ (build) a house near the sea.
2   We _____ (go) to an island last week.
3   My dad _____ (buy) me a bike yesterday.
4   I _____ (see) my friends on Saturday.
5   I _____ (get up) at 7 o'clock this morning.
6   They _____ (give) him a nice photo album.
7   Martha cooked a pizza and _____ (eat) it.
8   Sam and Ben _____ (catch) a fish in the river.

D **Write.**

| buy | build | catch | eat | ~~get up~~ | go |

1

I ___got up___ at 7 o'clock.

4

Tina _____ a new bag.

2

They _____ to the Pyramids last summer.

5

Tom and Paul _____ fish by the river.

3

Bobby _____ a big pizza.

6

We _____ a house in the village.

E **Read and draw. Then say.**

Last year, I went to the Pyramids. I saw lots of camels.

A Write.

American   English   Greek   Japanese   ~~Spanish~~

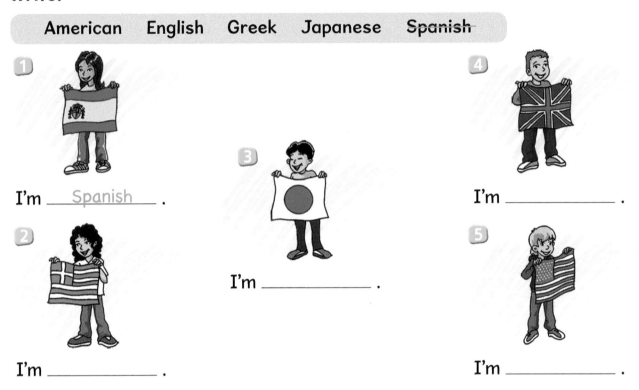

1 I'm ___Spanish___ .

2 I'm _____ .

3 I'm _____ .

4 I'm _____ .

5 I'm _____ .

B Find, circle and write.

```
Q E N V Y B W H P H
Q V L R E G Q O G D
I C R Q U R A K L E
B K C K X E X U K N
J A P A N E S E V G
N L M U N K E Q S L
J P S M A O Y E H I
A M E R I C A N C S
Y B J S P A N I S H
G O L D M E D A L R
```

1 American

4 _____

2 _____

5 _____

3 _____

6 _____

72

C **Match.**

1 They didn't have pizza for lunch. ☐ d

2 We didn't go on holiday to Japan. ☐

3 Carly and Sammy didn't go to the cinema. ☐

4 Mum didn't buy bananas. ☐

5 Paul didn't play ice hockey. ☐

6 She didn't get up at 7 o'clock. ☐

D **Write.**

1 Victor caught a big fish! He _____didn't catch_____ a small fish.

2 The Inuits built igloos. They _____ pyramids.

3 Alan stayed at home. He _____ in a hotel.

4 Jenny ate rice. She _____ chips.

5 Mary won a gold medal! She _____ a silver medal.

6 Grandpa got up at 6 o'clock. He _____ at 5 o'clock.

E **Write about you. Then draw and colour.**

I am Maria. I'm Spanish.
I play ice hockey.

73

Lesson 1

A **Write.**

 g o s t r a i g h t a h e a d

 t _ r _ l _ f _

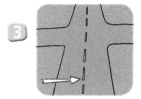 _ r _ s _ the r _ a _

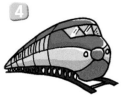 t _ a _ n

 _ u _ n l _ f _

 t _ a _ n _ t _ t _ o _

 _ i _ n

B **Write.**

cross the road   go straight ahead   sign   train
train station   turn left   turn right

1   go straight ahead

2 _____

3 _____

4 _____

5 _____

6 _____

7 _____

C Circle.

1 Did you buy a scooter?
(Yes, I did.) / No, I didn't.

2 Did he catch a fish?
Yes, he did. / No, he didn't.

3 Did Mum go on the train?
Yes, she did. / No, she didn't.

4 Did they win the game?
Yes, they did. / No, they didn't.

5 Did the cat eat the fish?
Yes, it did. / No, it didn't.

6 Did you pack the map?
Yes, I did. / No, I didn't.

D Write.

1   Did you have fish and chips?
2   Did the kids do their homework?
3   Did Mary look at her map?
4   Did the train come at 7 o'clock?
5   Did you have a French lesson today?
6   Did Bill play football today?

a   No, they didn't
b   Yes, he did.
c   Yes, it did.
d   No, I didn't.
e   Yes, we did.
f   No, she didn't.

E Write and say.

cross   left   ~~museum~~   straight   turn

Can you tell me the way
to the ___museum___?

Of course! Go _____ ahead.
_____ right and
_____ the road.
Then, turn _____!

Lesson 2

A Circle.

1
That (seal)/ cage
is so cute!

2
Look! The bird is
ill / free now!

3
Open / Free the
window. It's hot!

4
'Cage / Call Grandma,
please Tom!'

5
'Is Tweety in her
cage / open?'

6
Jack is in bed.
He's call / ill.

B Write.

1 An animal that is not in a cage.   f _r_ e _e_
2 This is when you feel bad.   i _ l
3 You use a telephone to do this.   c _ l _
4 These animals live on the beach.   _ e _ l
5 You can keep a canary in this.   _ a _ e
6 You can do this to a door or window.   _ p _ n

C Write.

1 I am going to play football.
   I'm going to play football.

2 They are going to walk to school.
   _____

3 He is going to help his grandma.
   _____

4 We are going to watch a film.
   _____

5 You are going to eat some cake!
   _____

D **Write.**

1

We ___'re going to make___ a sandwich!

2

Our kitten's ill. I _____ _____ a vet!

3

This room is messy! You _____ it.

4

It's her birthday! She _____ _____ a goldfish.

E **Write and say.**

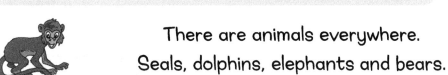

There are animals everywhere.
Seals, dolphins, elephants and bears.
Some are _____ill_____ or have nowhere to stay.
We must help the animals today!
Let's all try to be more _____,
Because the forests and seas aren't clean.

Save our animals!
Penguins and _____ .
Meerkats and whales.
Together we must find a way.
_____ our animals today!

Save our animals!
_____ and lions.
Monkeys and frogs.
Together we _____ find a way.
Save our animals today!

A Match.

clean

dirty

drop litter

plant

nature

start a fire

B Circle and write.

1 They ____started a fire____ in the forest!
   a cleaned a fire
   b started a fire

2 Let's _____ a tree!
   a drop
   b plant

3 The beaches are _____ .
   a clean
   b dirty

4 Please help us save _____ .
   a nature
   b litter

5 The dog is very _____!
   a dirty
   b clean

6 I saw them _____ in the street.
   a drop litter
   b plant trees

78

C Circle.

1 I 'm not going to / isn't going to have lunch now.

2 They aren't going to / isn't going to go shopping.

3 You aren't going to / 'm not going to catch a train.

4 Ruby aren't going to / isn't going to buy flowers.

5 It 'm not going to / isn't going to rain a lot this summer.

6 We aren't going to / isn't going to pack our suitcases now.

D Write.

1 We _____aren't going to_____ take an umbrella!

2 Susie _____ make any biscuits today.

3 I _____ do my homework now.

4 You _____ go to your piano lesson today.

5 Bill and Barry _____ dance at the party.

6 Dad _____ play football on Saturday.

E Write and say.

clean   litter   nature   trees   start

My name's Patty. I LOVE _____nature_____ ! I'm going to _____ the beach every Saturday and plant _____ too. I'm not going to drop _____ or _____ fires. Those things make me sad!

79

A Find, circle and write.

G	L	M	L	E	D	J	R
J	D	N	M	D	K	S	H
D	G	R	N	U	B	H	P
R	P	U	X	C	A	O	V
A	T	M	Q	O	R	W	K
W	V	E	B	M	K	V	Z
K	P	E	E	I	X	Q	F
R	V	T	M	C	A	B	M

1 bark

2

3

4

5

B Write.

bark   cartoons   comics   draw   meet   show

1   Is that dog going to _____bark_____ all night?

2   Let's go to that car _____ on Friday!

3   I am going to _____ a picture of an elephant.

4   Sam loves to read _____ on Sunday morning.

5   My uncle draws amazing _____!

6   I'm going to _____ my cousin at the train station.

C **Write.**

1 Is he going to win the gold medal?

✔ _____Yes, he is_____ .

2 Am I going to clean the house?

✔ _____ .

3 Are they going to cross the road?

✗ _____ .

4 Is she going to have fish for breakfast?

✗ _____ .

5 Are we going to clean the cage?

✔ _____ .

6 Is he going to play tennis with his friends?

✗ _____ .

D **Write.**

1 ___Is Helen going to buy___ (Helen / buy) a new sweater?

2 _____ (you / go) to school?

3 _____ (Milly / play) a computer game?

4 _____ (Dad / call) the vet?

5 _____ (Sue / have) a party?

6 _____ (he / stay) at home today?

E **Write and say.**

Jen and Bill

Paul

The boys

Fluffy

Julie

1 Are Jen and Bill going to eat a pizza?

2 Is Paul going to do his homework?

3 Are the boys going to plant a tree?

4 Is Fluffy going to drink the water?

5 Is Julie going to draw a picture?

a No, they aren't.

b Yes, it is.

c Yes, they are.

d No, she isn't.

e No, he isn't.

A Write.

¹P	A	S	S	²P	O	R	T

³F
A
A
G

⁴A

⁵G

B Write.

Come on! Let's go on the ___ghost train___!

You need a _____ to go to America.

She's at the _____ . Her plane leaves at 10 o'clock.

Don't worry! I'll send you a _____!

They live in a _____ not a house!

C **Write.**

1 ___I'll show___ (show) you my new comic.

2 My brother _____ (draw) you a picture.

3 We _____ (go) to Disney World next year.

4 Mary and John _____ (move) to their new flat in August.

5 She _____ (watch) her favourite TV show.

6 They _____ (take) us to the tallest building in London!

D **Write.**

1 I will go swimming on Saturday.
  I'll go swimming on Saturday.

2 She will write a postcard.
  _____

3 They will go on the ghost train later.
  _____

4 You will live in a flat next year.
  _____

5 He will make a sandwich for lunch.
  _____

6 We will go to France next year.
  _____

E **Write and say.**

We'll see you in
S _ p _t_ em _be_ r, Mr Smith.
We'll see you in
September, Mrs Jones.

We can't stay.
We're on _ o _ i _ a _ .
So bye bye!
See you later.
Off we go!

Let's do the holiday hop!
_ o _ on your left foot.
Hop on your right foot.
Then t _ r _ left and now
turn right.
C _ a _ your hands.
And jump up high.

Come on, boys and girls!
Let's do the holiday hop!

A Write.

1 I often  <u>go sightseeing</u> with my parents on holiday.

2 I write in my  _____ every day.

3 It's not a very long  _____ .

4 Dad gave me the  _____ for a computer game.

5 I'm going to  _____ to my friend.

B Write.

t <u>r</u> <u>i</u> p

_ o _ _ _ _

d _ a _ y

g _ s _ _ _ t s _ e _ n g

w _ i _ e

C Write.

1

I'll eat ice cream.

I __won't eat__ chips.

2

He'll go on the big wheel.

He _____ on the ghost train.

3

We'll read comics.

We _____ books.

4

She'll play with the kitten.

She _____ the dog.

D Write.

1 I _____won't do_____ (do) my homework now. I'm tired!

2 Sally _____ (go) shopping tomorrow.

3 Mark and Will _____ (play) football on Sunday.

4 Mum _____ (cook) at the weekends!

5 My brother _____ (read) comics.

6 Jane _____ (visit) her grandma this week.

E Write and say.

~~How are you?~~
I'll go swimming.
I won't go
sightseeing.
I'm in Spain.

Hi! Jackie,

How are you?

_____

_____

_____

Bye for now.

Steve

85

Review 4

A Write.

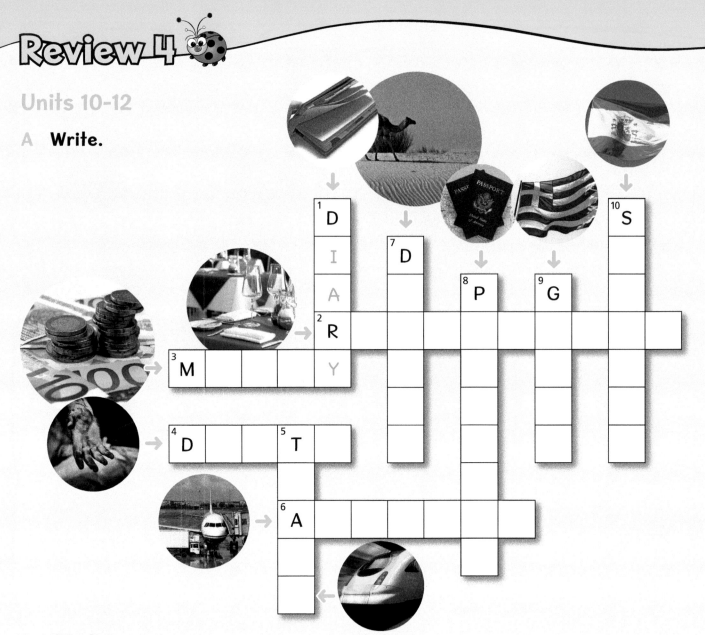

B Circle.

1 I'm going to (open) / free the window.

2 My pyramid / suitcase was heavy!

3 Pete's going to read a train / comic.

4 I'll watch a cage / cartoon on TV later.

5 Ronaldo is a famous football player / postcard.

6 Chris lived in a flat / building not a house.

C Write.

1 umbrella / not / going / to / an / buy / I'm   _I'm not going to buy an umbrella._

2 draw / we / are / ? / to / going   _____

3 going / she's / watch / to / film / a   _____

4 ski / ? / is / going / to / she   _____

5 they're / vet / to / call / a / going   _____

86

D Write.

1 My mum _____gave_____ (give) me a diary last week.

2 I _____ (study) for three hours yesterday.

3 Fred _____ (not catch) a fish.

4 _____ Sam _____ (do) her homework? No, she didn't.

5 _____ you _____ (get) the passports? Yes, I did.

6 I _____ (not see) any camels in the desert.

E Circle.

He will / won't write a postcard.

Harry will / won't read his comic now.

Pat will / won't visit his grandparents on Saturday.

Mum and Dad will / won't go sightseeing tomorrow.

Jane will / won't pack the suitcase now.

F Write about you.

'My weekend'

I will ....

I won't ....

87

Wordsearches

Unit 1

Find, circle and write 12 words from Unit 1.

```
Q V M A O L D P Y I
Y A U Y D P U J D R
O U G F Z S T A R S
U N L O E I Y H U C
N T Y R M S Y U N A
G E E E A A D X C M
C O U S I N E W L E
V M X T L D V F E L
P C U T E S L L B D
G X U Z Q G P O F E
```

1 _____aunt_____
2 _____
3 _____
4 _____
5 _____
6 _____
7 _____
8 _____
9 _____
10 _____
11 _____
12 _____

Unit 2

Find, circle and write 12 words from Unit 2.

```
F L M W N A W H P C
M E P L Q C I O R P
C O U A S R N R K A
A P P M L O G N I T
N A P P I B P V T E
A R Y D P A A T T A
R D I S P T A V E P
Y K X B E G A R N O
B R A O R E F U R T
E V J N S S W I N G
```

1 _____acrobat_____
2 _____
3 _____
4 _____
5 _____
6 _____
7 _____
8 _____
9 _____
10 _____
11 _____
12 _____

Find, circle and write 12 words from Unit 3.

U	B	E	L	T	S	Q	E	K	G
V	P	G	L	F	W	A	L	L	D
Q	X	C	I	O	E	C	Q	B	O
L	V	F	K	U	A	O	N	E	O
G	T	L	H	N	T	A	E	T	R
L	J	O	C	T	E	T	A	W	O
O	V	O	M	A	R	H	R	E	L
V	N	R	G	I	V	U	V	E	J
E	U	B	E	N	C	H	W	N	W
S	E	T	O	Y	B	O	X	E	A

1 _____ belt _____
2 _____
3 _____
4 _____
5 _____
6 _____
7 _____
8 _____
9 _____
10 _____
11 _____
12 _____

Find, circle and write 12 words from Unit 4.

O	I	Y	J	N	Z	F	M	K	Y
C	A	V	U	O	S	E	A	C	M
T	U	D	L	V	E	B	Y	E	F
O	G	Y	Y	E	P	R	A	M	N
B	U	C	H	M	T	U	P	A	B
E	S	L	T	B	E	A	R	R	Z
R	T	A	D	E	M	R	I	C	N
J	U	N	E	R	B	Y	L	H	H
G	V	D	E	C	E	M	B	E	R
J	A	N	U	A	R	Y	X	C	E

1 _____ April _____
2 _____
3 _____
4 _____
5 _____
6 _____
7 _____
8 _____
9 _____
10 _____
11 _____
12 _____

Wordsearches

Unit 5

Find, circle and write 12 words from Unit 5.

```
U F T H O T E L M X
L W H B F I R S T Q
R T I S E V E N T H
K R R K T F I F T H
S A D Q O X V G L C
E I S E I G H T H K
C N I N T H N P L R
O E A G F O R T H R
N R T E N T H X V Q
D S I X T H D I K H
```

1 _____eighth_____
2 _____
3 _____
4 _____
5 _____
6 _____
7 _____
8 _____
9 _____
10 _____
11 _____
12 _____

Unit 6

Find, circle and write 12 words from Unit 6.

```
T X W C L D Q C F R
A S R H E B Z W I G
B A G I M K I S Z B
L N R P O H P U Z F
E D A S N N I G Y O
F W S E A I Z A D R
I I S D D N Z R R T
F C Q Z E E A S I Y
T H E P Q T N X N P
Y R J A M Y E P K F
```

1 _____chips_____
2 _____
3 _____
4 _____
5 _____
6 _____
7 _____
8 _____
9 _____
10 _____
11 _____
12 _____

Find, circle and write 12 words from Unit 7.

P	D	B	I	S	C	U	I	T	D
E	A	R	R	O	W	C	Z	A	O
X	C	U	D	X	H	Q	H	J	C
C	A	S	T	R	O	N	A	U	T
I	A	C	T	O	R	I	S	C	O
T	B	V	N	B	O	W	C	P	R
E	C	E	W	J	G	L	A	I	D
D	O	T	X	K	J	W	R	L	K
P	O	S	T	M	A	N	E	O	C
V	K	T	F	Y	A	J	D	T	K

1 _actor_
2 _____
3 _____
4 _____
5 _____
6 _____
7 _____
8 _____
9 _____
10 _____
11 _____
12 _____

Find, circle and write 12 words from Unit 8.

K	S	V	N	Z	L	X	Z	U	F
I	B	L	A	R	G	E	U	Y	X
D	C	T	S	N	O	W	M	A	N
S	U	N	N	Y	W	G	B	H	S
L	S	O	L	D	I	E	R	E	C
E	B	W	M	F	N	L	E	A	A
E	N	K	V	N	D	I	L	D	R
P	B	F	B	U	Y	S	L	U	Y
Y	L	I	T	T	L	E	A	A	W
K	D	G	B	U	T	T	O	N	S

1 _button_
2 _____
3 _____
4 _____
5 _____
6 _____
7 _____
8 _____
9 _____
10 _____
11 _____
12 _____

Wordsearches

Unit 9

Find, circle and write 12 words from Unit 9.

```
A  W  B  T  F  U  V  S  O  M
H  O  O  P  R  C  Y  T  W  M
O  M  N  L  I  H  F  R  D  E
M  Z  E  A  E  I  V  O  I  A
E  E  Q  N  N  S  C  N  N  T
F  A  U  T  D  T  L  G  O  S
Q  R  E  L  L  O  O  Z  S  D
V  T  E  Y  Y  R  C  D  A  E
Y  H  N  S  B  Y  K  B  U  Q
D  D  A  R  K  T  C  I  R  Y
```

1 _____ bone _____
2 _____
3 _____
4 _____
5 _____
6 _____
7 _____
8 _____
9 _____
10 _____
11 _____
12 _____

Unit 10

Find, circle and write 12 words from Unit 10.

```
S  R  I  C  E  C  L  U  P  M
P  H  E  A  V  Y  M  F  Y  B
A  C  L  U  S  E  G  D  R  U
N  P  G  R  E  E  K  E  A  I
I  S  P  A  C  K  M  S  M  L
S  U  I  T  C  A  S  E  I  D
H  Z  M  C  C  C  E  R  D  I
M  P  L  A  Y  E  R  T  P  N
W  F  A  M  O  U  S  S  K  G
G  P  E  N  G  L  I  S  H  B
```

1 _____ building _____
2 _____
3 _____
4 _____
5 _____
6 _____
7 _____
8 _____
9 _____
10 _____
11 _____
12 _____

92

Find, circle and write 12 words from Unit 11.

```
D  G  H  D  I  R  T  Y  X  F
T  R  A  I  N  C  C  C  N  R
I  L  L  C  Y  A  L  Y  A  E
Z  J  S  D  Y  L  E  P  T  E
C  B  J  E  N  L  A  L  U  W
S  D  O  X  K  C  N  A  R  N
I  F  S  Y  S  A  K  N  E  W
G  R  G  Y  E  G  X  T  I  W
N  V  H  F  A  E  Q  X  B  C
D  G  N  X  L  F  O  P  E  N
```

1 cage
2 _____
3 _____
4 _____
5 _____
6 _____
7 _____
8 _____
9 _____
10 _____
11 _____
12 _____

Find, circle and write 12 words from Unit 12.

```
C  C  G  A  C  O  M  I  C  N
K  P  M  I  H  N  I  M  P  N
V  O  Y  R  T  H  F  O  A  M
K  S  P  P  D  O  L  N  S  E
B  T  E  O  Q  R  A  E  S  E
A  C  D  R  A  W  T  Y  P  T
R  A  C  T  K  S  R  V  O  S
K  R  A  K  N  P  I  F  R  H
Z  D  X  U  S  P  P  U  T  O
O  D  D  I  A  R  Y  V  P  W
```

1 airport
2 _____
3 _____
4 _____
5 _____
6 _____
7 _____
8 _____
9 _____
10 _____
11 _____
12 _____

Jigsaw Puzzles

Notes

Notes

Notes

Notes